The Labrador Retriever

by Suzanne Lord
Edited by Julie Bach

CRESTWOOD HOUSE
New York
Collier Macmillan Canada
Toronto
Maxwell Macmillan International Publishing Group
New York   Oxford   Singapore   Sydney

LIBRARY OF CONGRESS CATALOGING-IN-PUBLICATION DATA

Lord, Suzanne, 1946–
    The Labrador retriever / by Suzanne Lord ; edited by Julie Bach.
  – 1st ed.
      p.   cm. — (Top dog series)
    Summary: Discusses the history, physical characteristics, care, and breeding of the Labrador retriever.
    ISBN 0-89686-526-6
      1. Labrador retriever—Juvenile literature. [1. Labrador retriever. 2. Dogs.] I. Bach, Julie S., 1963– . II. Title.
    III. Series: Top dog (Crestwood House)
    SF429.L3L67   1990
    636.7′52—dc20
                               90-34198
                                 CIP
                                 AC

PHOTO CREDITS

Cover: Notinghil Labradors: (Diane and Gabriel Barletta)
Peter Arnold, Inc.: (Gerard Lacz) 4, 42
Ruth Gardner: 6
Second Sight: 9
Reynolds Photography: (Larry Reynolds) 10, 12, 27, 41
Notinghil Labradors: (Diane and Gabriel Barletta) 14, 17, 21, 23, 32
Cedarhill Labradors: (Thomas J. Feneis) 18, 29
Barber Photo Studios: (Bob Barber) 24
J. Sun Farms Labradors: (Terry M. DePietro) 31, 36, 38, 45
Terry Gains: 35

CRESTWOOD HOUSE

Macmillan Publishing Company
866 Third Avenue
New York, NY 10022

Collier Macmillan Canada, Inc.
1200 Eglinton Avenue East
Suite 200
Don Mills, Ontario M3C 3N1

Printed in the United States of America
First Edition

10 9 8 7 6 5 4 3 2 1

◢CONTENTS

For more information about Labrador retrievers, write to:

Labrador Retriever Club
Dr. Bernard Ziessow, Secretary
32695 Redfern
Franklin, MI 48025

THE PERFECT DOG

In the 1920s, a new *breed* of dog—the Labrador retriever—was introduced to the United States. Before long, people realized that this dog could do much more than hunt game and be a good pet. This beautiful, friendly dog could do almost any task people asked of it.

For instance, during World War II, Labrador retrievers carried important messages for the armed services. They sniffed out mines and booby traps. They found unexploded bombs. Labradors were even taught to parachute! They jumped from airplanes to help U.S. soldiers.

Police forces began to use Labradors, too. The dogs were good at tracking down criminals and finding hidden illegal drugs. They're still used by police forces today.

Labradors are very helpful in disasters. They can be trained to obey hand signals, and they aren't frightened by loud noises. They will run through broken glass, dust, or smoke to find people who are hurt. Frightened victims can tell that a Labrador is coming to help—not to bite them!

5

Labradors not only make excellent pets, but they are also useful in tracking down criminals and guiding the blind.

Labradors are also used as "therapy" dogs. In nursing homes, people feel less lonely if they have a big, friendly dog to pet. People in mental hospitals are helped by the affection Labradors give so freely. In children's hospitals, Labradors can fetch something dropped by a child in a wheelchair or hospital bed.

Labradors also make excellent *Seeing Eye dogs* for blind people. They are smart, loving, and easy to train. They are dependable. They

Labradors are friendly and affectionate. They rarely pick a fight.

always want to protect their owners from danger. Also—very important for blind people—they can make decisions on their own without being told what to do. No wonder many owners think the Labrador retriever is the world's most perfect dog.

MISTAKEN IDENTITY

If you were asked where Labrador retrievers came from, what would you guess? Labrador? That's what most people would say. Labrador is a small area on the eastern mainland of Canada. Very close to it is an island called Newfoundland. About 150 years ago, somebody mistakenly said this breed of retriever was from Labrador. But it really came from the island of Newfoundland! Labradors aren't from Labrador at all!

Labradors have always been retrievers. Their thick coats were perfect for hunting in the cold Newfoundland waters. But they didn't retrieve birds as they do now. Early Labradors retrieved fish. The dogs helped cod fishers bring in their fishing nets. The dogs grabbed different parts of the heavy nets and pulled them ashore. They also caught stray cod that fell back into the sea. And they retrieved equipment dropped overboard.

Labradors were brought to England some time around the early 1820s. British bird hunters were delighted. They could see right away what fine, eager-to-please retrievers these dogs were.

Labradors were the pride of British hunters for a hundred years. Then, in the late 1920s, American hunters in England brought the dogs to the United States. Soon Labradors were recognized as a breed by the American Kennel Club. The first American Labrador retriever club was started in the 1930s. The first show for Labradors was held in 1934.

Throughout their long history, Labradors have had many famous owners. In England, King George VI owned champion Labradors. And when Averell Harriman became governor of New York in 1955, his Labradors moved into the governor's mansion right along with him.

One of the most important jobs a Labrador can do is act as a Seeing Eye dog.

THE LABRADOR IN CLOSE-UP

Labrador retrievers can be one of three colors—black, yellow, or chocolate. Some black Labradors have a small spot of white on their chests. Chocolate-colored Labradors range from deep chocolate to light sedge. Yellow Labradors are not always yellow. Their color ranges from light cream to fox red. Labradors' eyes can be anywhere from clear yellow to light brown or black.

Male Labradors stand between 22½ and 24½ inches tall at the *withers*. They weigh between 60 and 75 pounds. Females are about an inch shorter and five pounds lighter than males. A Labrador's head is well shaped. If it is healthy and well bred, its cheeks have no fleshiness. Its neck has no loose skin under the jaws. Its medium-sized ears hang close to the head. A Labrador has strong teeth.

A Labrador also has a powerful chest that is wide and deep, and its back is sturdy.

A Labrador's tail is like no other dog's. It is called an otter tail because of its shape. It's not feathered, like other dogs' tails. Instead, it is covered with the same kind of coat that is on

11

Labradors have two coats of fur that help them stay warm and dry.

the rest of the dog. A Labrador carries its tail high, but not curled up over its back. The way it carries its tail gives it an alert look.

A Labrador has two coats of fur. That's why it can stay warm in cold water. The outer coat is short and very dense. The hairs are usually straight and stiff. The second coat, called the undercoat, is very important because it's waterproof. It insulates the dog from wetness and cold temperatures. This coat is thick and fluffy.

Dog lovers describe the Labrador as balanced. Every part of a fine Labrador fits together, without any one part standing out.

A FRIENDLY PERSONALITY

Labradors are popular because they're such friendly, eager dogs. They appeal to almost everyone. They're good pets. They're good retrievers. They're good workers. You can keep a Labrador in the city or in the country. If you have to go on vacation, your Labrador will do well in a kennel while you're away. Labradors also get along with other pets—even kittens and horses.

Labradors are popular pets because they get along with every member of the family—even the cat.

Labradors get along with other dogs. This black Lab patiently listens to its yellow friend.

Labradors are not aggressive. That's why they haven't been trained as attack dogs for police forces. But they are good watchdogs. Your Labrador will always let you know when a stranger comes to your house.

Many people like Labradors because they don't bark all the time. They're not snappish. A Labrador will defend itself if it has to, but it's not likely to start a fight.

Labradors are obedient. They are easy to train, as long as they know what's expected of them. They are eager to learn. They're intelligent, and they have good memories. And when you teach them a trick, they'll love showing it off.

Most of all, Labradors are affectionate. They are loyal and reliable. If you give your Labrador a lot of love, you'll get it all back—and more!

CHOOSING A LABRADOR PUPPY

Choosing a puppy can be very exciting, but try not to let excitement overcome common sense. You want to choose a healthy puppy that will grow up to be the right dog for you.

First, you need to decide what kind of a Labrador you want. Do you want a champion that will win competitions? Do you want a top-notch hunting dog? Or do you want a lovable pet? A dog bred from champion parents will cost more than a dog bred to be a pet. If you decide to buy a pet, you may have to sign an agreement that you won't breed your dog.

Second, you need to decide whether you want a male or female dog. Some people think male dogs are a little more aggressive than females. Females go into *heat* twice a year and have to be kept safe from male dogs in the neighborhood. If you want to breed puppies, then of course you need a female. You might also want to decide ahead of time what color Labrador you like best.

Once you've made these decisions, look for a good *breeder* in your area. A *veterinarian* or the American Kennel Association can help you find one. It is often better to buy from a breeder than a pet store. Breeders may be more expensive and not as close to your home, but they know a lot about the puppies they're selling. They also may have more than one *litter* for you to look at.

When you arrive at the breeder's, look at all the puppies he or she has. Also look carefully at the parents. Your puppy will probably look like its mother or father when it is full-grown. Watch the litter for a while. Look for puppies that are playful. Avoid ones that seem listless or shy. Reach out to touch a puppy you like. Is it friendly?

Ask the breeder lots of questions. Make sure the puppy you choose is healthy. Most breeders will let you take your puppy to a veterinarian before the sale is final.

One more thing to consider before you make your decision is that Labradors often have a

Because Labradors are gentle and patient, they make good pets for small children.

disease called *hip dysplasia*. It is passed on from their parents. The breeder should have a paper saying that your puppy's mother and father don't have the disease. If you can't get the paper, buy from another breeder.

The breeder of your puppy will give you its *pedigree*. These papers tell you about your puppy's ancestors. You should also get a record of your puppy's shots and details about its diet. You can then feed it the same food the breeder has been giving it. Once you're ready, you can take your puppy to its new home.

Choosing one puppy out of a litter can be a difficult decision.

CARING FOR YOUR LABRADOR

Try to imagine your house from your puppy's point of view. It's a big, strange place that may even seem a little scary at first. With your help, though, this big house will soon be its happy home.

A puppy needs all the same things a human baby needs when it's brought home from the hospital: a place to sleep, food, water, and lots of love.

At first, you'll want your puppy to sleep inside the house. You may even want to let it sleep in your bedroom. Make a special bed on the floor for it. It may cry the first night because it is lonely for its mother and litter-mates. Don't let it sleep with you. You'll soon have a full-grown dog sleeping in your bed, and you won't be able to make it leave. Instead, give your puppy a soft toy, or wrap a ticking clock in a blanket. These things will remind the puppy of its mother and its littermates.

When your puppy is older, decide whether it will live mostly indoors or outdoors. If your dog is going to live outside, it should have a doghouse. The house has to be big enough for your dog to move around in it. It also has to be kept clean. Raise the doghouse off the ground. This will keep it well insulated. In the winter, you will want to add extra bedding to keep your dog warm. You may also want to make the doghouse a little more snug to keep out drafts. When your dog isn't inside its doghouse, it will need a fenced yard in which to play.

If your puppy is an indoor dog, provide a bed in a warm place. You might want to dogproof your home. Make sure none of your houseplants are poisonous to dogs. Don't let your puppy chew on electrical wires. Keep sharp objects out of the dog's reach.

When you bring your puppy home, feed it the same food the breeder was feeding it. At first your puppy will eat several small meals a day. Gradually it will eat fewer, larger meals. Finally it will need only one big meal in the evening. Don't give your puppy bones to chew unless you're sure the bones won't splinter. Chicken and fish bones are especially bad. Most dogs like people food, but you shouldn't give your dog too much. It will get fat. Always keep your dog's water dish full of fresh water.

Labradors need plenty of exercise. Play with your dog every day. Wrestle and tumble with it. This will keep it alert and fit. But let your dog

This young Labrador is tired out after a day of hard exercise.

know that play doesn't include biting. Walk your Labrador at least once a day. Don't forget to clean up after your dog in residential areas.

Labradors don't need a lot of *grooming.* They usually keep themselves very clean. Brush your dog once a week with a soft hairbrush. When it sheds, brush it more often. Keep fleas and ticks away from your dog with a flea collar.

Giving a big dog a bath can be quite an adventure! But it's something you'll need to do once or twice a year. Use a large tub and warm—not hot—water. Keep soap out of your dog's eyes and ears. Use a special dog shampoo and rinse well. When your dog jumps out of the tub to shake itself off, watch out! Rub your dog dry with a big towel. You can dry it with a blow dryer, too. Just be careful not to burn your dog's hair or skin.

Take your dog to a veterinarian at least once a year. Do this even if your dog seems fine. Your vet will clean your dog's teeth and make sure it's healthy. Keep track of when your dog needs vaccination shots and boosters. A vet will help you. These shots keep your dog free from diseases like distemper and rabies. Your vet will also help keep your dog free of *worms*.

Your dog's regular checkups are important. Between checkups, keep an eye on your dog's health. Do you notice anything unusual? Runny eyes, patchy coat, a skin rash? If so, take your dog to the vet right away. Your dog depends on you to keep it healthy.

A WELL-TRAINED PET

Labradors love to learn and they love to please. If you let your Labrador puppy know what's right and wrong, both of you will be a lot happier. You'll have a well-trained dog that listens to you and loves you. Your dog will have an owner who won't let it get into trouble.

First you'll want to *housebreak* your puppy. Choose a place in the yard where you want it to go to relieve itself. Take it to the place after it eats or wakes up from a nap. Pet it and praise it when it uses the right spot. Soon your puppy will understand what to do. Of course, your puppy will relieve itself in the house a few times. Don't be angry. Clean up the mess so

A well-trained Lab will obey its owner's commands.

your puppy won't use that spot again. Go on with your training.

You'll also have to teach your puppy not to chew your belongings. Buy a few sturdy chew toys. When your puppy chews its toys, praise it. When it chews the furniture, scold it. Never hit your puppy, of course, but let it know that chewing the couch or your mother's slippers is not okay! Your puppy will soon grow out of its chewing stage.

Labradors are smart. You can begin teaching your puppy simple commands when it's only

The first commands your Labrador should learn are "come," "sit," and "stay."

four months old. Keep the training sessions short. A puppy can pay attention for only a few minutes.

Use the same commands all the time. And use them over and over. Try not to confuse your puppy. Use a tone of voice that makes sense. If you have to scold your puppy, use a scolding voice. If you praise it, use a happy voice.

Maybe you're not sure you know how to train a puppy. You may want to take your dog to an obedience school. Both you and your dog can learn a lot from these classes.

If you do train your dog at home, start with an easy command. Teach your dog "come." Put its dish down. Then say its name and call "Come!" Later, use the same command without the dish. Repeat the command often in different places. Soon your dog will come every time you call it.

You can teach your dog other commands such as "sit," "lie down," and "stay." You can also teach it to *heel* when it walks. To do this, you'll need a leash and a *choke chain*. A choke chain won't really choke your dog. It closes tightly around its neck when you pull it. As soon as your dog heels, ease up on your leash. Your smart Labrador will soon understand what you want. Then you can use a regular collar.

You may want to carry dog treats with you during training. Give your dog a treat and lots of praise when it does well. Your dog will learn quickly. And it will love you for taking good care of it.

BREEDING A LABRADOR RETRIEVER

If you have a female Labrador, or *bitch*, you may want to breed her. People breed dogs to produce fine animals. They don't breed them just to have loads of puppies. They usually don't breed them to make money. Breeding is hard work and can be expensive. Make sure this is something you really want to do.

Of course, you don't have to breed your female Labrador. Your veterinarian can *spay* her. This simple operation prevents your dog from ever getting pregnant. It costs about $100. You can also make sure your male dog doesn't make another dog pregnant. Your vet can *neuter* him. That operation costs about the same as spaying.

Breeding champion Labradors requires careful planning.

If you do decide to breed your dog, your veterinarian or the Labrador Retriever Club can help you find a good mate, or *stud*, for your dog. Make sure both dogs are healthy. Check for hip dysplasia and other diseases. Look for a quality stud that will pass on good traits to your puppies.

The owner of the stud may charge a "stud fee." Or you may give the owner "pick of the litter." That means the owner gets the best puppy from your litter for free.

Breeders say you should not mate a Labrador during her first heat. She's too young. Wait until she's two years old. Then, when she's in her second week of heat and ready to become pregnant, take her to a stud male. If possible, have the dogs mate twice, a couple of days apart. This doubles the Labrador's chances of getting pregnant. Keep the female away from other dogs at this time. You don't want her to mate again because she may end up with a mixed litter.

If you want a certain color Lab, breed your female to a stud of that color. But don't be surprised if your puppies are a color you didn't expect. Two black Labs can have a yellow puppy. Pairs of chocolate Labs have been known to have chocolate, black, and yellow puppies, all in the same litter!

A LITTER OF PUPPIES

Your pregnant Labrador needs special care. Take her for lots of short, easy walks. After about six weeks, don't let her jump around too much. Talk to a vet about a special diet. That might include vitamins and extra food. She needs lots of nourishment while she's pregnant.

A Lab nurses her young—all eight of them!

Your dog's pregnancy will last about 60 days. A few weeks before she's ready to deliver, prepare a quiet place for her. Make a *whelping box* out of cardboard or wood. Line it with newspapers and maybe an old blanket. You'll have to change the newspaper frequently once the puppies are born.

As your dog gets closer to delivering, she may do some unusual things. She may lose her appetite and want to be left alone. She might pant and shiver. Her temperature will probably be lower than normal. Don't worry about these changes. They're all natural.

The birth of new puppies is a beautiful thing to watch. Most likely, your dog will not need any help. But you should be ready in case she has problems. Even if she's fine, she'll appreciate some encouraging words and a few pats on the head.

Your Lab will let you know when it's time. She'll lie down in her box and begin straining. The puppies will be born one at a time, each in its own *birth sac*. When the first puppy arrives, the mother will cut it out of its sac with her teeth. She'll lick it to make it start breathing. She'll also bite off the puppy's *umbilical cord*. The other puppies will be born about 30 minutes apart. Soon all the puppies will be nudging their mother's *teats* for their first meal.

Puppies in a Labrador litter may be black, yellow, or chocolate. This yellow pup has two black siblings.

If your dog has trouble with the delivery, help her out. You may have to take a birth sac off a puppy yourself. You may have to cut its cord if the mother doesn't. Use a pair of sterilized scissors. Have a warm towel ready for rubbing the puppies dry.

The mother will probably eat the *afterbirth.* This is normal. For a couple of days, she will need plenty of water and light meals. Your vet may also recommend extra calcium.

31

Let your dog and her puppies be quiet for a few weeks. Don't bring many people over to see them. Try not to handle the pups too much. Soon your dog will want to go outside. Then you can take care of her pups for her. You may want to trim their nails so they don't scratch their mother when they feed. Carefully pick up the puppies with both hands so you don't drop them.

At two and a half to three weeks, the pups can eat some solid food. Your vet will tell you what to feed them and how much. They'll still drink their mother's milk. But soon she'll *wean* them completely. Then they'll eat only puppy food.

Spend time with your puppies. Take good care of them. They'll learn from you how to relate to people. If you want to sell your puppies, register them with the American Kennel Club. Soon the time will come for your puppies to go to their new homes. Because of your hard work, they'll be healthy, happy pets.

Giving your puppy lots of attention, love, and care will help it grow into a happy, loyal pet.

SHOWING YOUR LABRADOR

One of the joys of owning a top-quality dog is entering it in dog shows. The American Kennel Club holds two kinds of dog shows: point shows and specialty shows.

In a point show, a dog is judged on how well it conforms to the standards for its breed. In a specialty show, the best dogs of the breed compete. Breeders go to these shows to see what new strains of Labradors are being produced.

Most owners start by entering their Labradors in a point show. It can be a lot of fun. You and your dog get to meet other dogs and owners. But you have to know some of the rules.

To enter a show, fill out an official entry form. Make sure you mail this form by the deadline. Read the form carefully. You can enter your dog in many different categories, or classes. You have to pay an entry fee for every event your dog enters.

There are puppy classes for owners who want to start showing their dogs early. Other classes include Novice, Bred-by-Exhibitor, and Open. These classes are for dogs who haven't won a first prize. There are also classes for dogs who have won first prizes. Maybe someday your dog will be in one of those.

Start training your dog early to get ready for the dog show. It will have to stand very still while the judges look it over. They'll even open its mouth and look at its teeth. Your dog will also have to trot beside you in a straight line with its head up. It may have to trot in a line with other dogs.

These champion Labs pose proudly with their owners.

A yellow, a chocolate, and a black await their next command.

The judges will look at your Lab to see how closely it matches the standards for the breed. If your dog wins three or more points, it becomes a major. If your dog wins two majors and 15 other points, it becomes a champion.

To become a champion, your dog will need all your help. Exercise it before the show. Don't feed it until afterward. Groom it carefully. Most of all, give it lots of love and encouragement. Don't be disappointed if your dog doesn't win its first show. It may take many shows to make a champion. In the meantime, enjoy watching your dog as it shows off all the fine qualities of a Labrador retriever.

TRAINING A TALENTED RETRIEVER

Labradors are excellent hunting dogs. They learn quickly and have fun pleasing their owners.

Start teaching your Labrador puppy to retrieve when it is three months old. Take your pup to an area where it cannot run away. Put the dog between your knees, facing out. Shake a sock full of feathers in front of its face. Then toss the sock in front of you. Urge the dog to fetch.

Your Labrador will run after the sock. But it may not understand that it's supposed to bring it back! Call your dog to you. If it comes, praise it and gently remove the sock from its mouth. But if the dog wants to play, don't chase it! You're not trying to teach it tug-of-war. When your dog has settled down, approach quietly. Tell it, "Leave," as you gently put your thumb and index finger on either side of your dog's mouth. This will make your dog give you the sock.

Help your Labrador get used to loud sounds. When hunting day comes, your retriever will have to sit quietly next to rifles being fired. Clap your hands often and loudly near your dog. Then your dog won't be gun-shy.

A Labrador rests under its owner's car between meets at a field trial.

Once your dog has learned to fetch, teach it to retrieve objects out of water. But never teach water retrieval in a swimming pool. Your dog might not be able to climb the steep sides of a pool.

Teach your Labrador to respond to both voice and hand signals. It must learn to use all its senses to find what it is looking for. It must be willing to jump into cold water and run through brambles and undergrowth. It must learn to find the fastest, best way to get where it is headed.

Always give your dog lots of praise when it brings you something—even if it's just a dead mouse. Eventually your dog will learn that you want it to bring the grouse you just shot.

Make sure you have plenty of time to train your retriever. A little training is worse than none. Have fun with your dog. It will look forward to this time with you. If you train your dog well, both of you will enjoy years of hunting. Who knows? Maybe your Lab will even win a hunting competition!

THE CHALLENGE OF A FIELD TRIAL

Perhaps your Labrador is an excellent retriever. If so, you might want to enter it in a *field trial*. Field trials are very different from dog shows. They test your dog's ability to hunt. Your dog's looks aren't important.

Joining a retriever field trial club is a good place to begin. These clubs lease land for training. There you can teach your dog to hunt. When the club hosts field trials, you and your dog can get some valuable experience.

Winning a field trial takes a lot of practice. Remember, the other dogs in the competition have been hunting just as long as yours has— maybe longer. Also, training a dog for field trials can be expensive.

Field trials can last up to three days. Dogs compete in stakes instead of classes. You must fill out an entry form and pay an entry fee. The trials are held outside, of course. It might be raining or cold, so be prepared. If the trial is far from your home, you'll need a place to stay for a few days.

Your dog will be required to retrieve on land and in the water. It may be competing against 25 to 80 dogs. Keep your nerves steady. Be enthusiastic and praise your dog often. Your Labrador will be eager to please you and show off all the things you've taught it. Together, you and your dog can enjoy the challenge of competition.

Jumping over hurdles is only part of a field trial. Dogs also have to retrieve decoys and pass obedience tests.

ANDA'S CHALLENGE

Esther had been waiting for the field trial for a long time. For years, she had been training her Labrador retriever, Anda, to hunt. Everybody said Anda was the best retriever they'd ever seen. Well, they'd soon find out. The three-day field trial was starting.

Esther had entered Anda in the amateur stake. She had filled out the entry form carefully and paid the fee. It was expensive, but it was worth it to see Anda compete. Esther was sure her dog would do well.

On the first day of competition, 75 dogs were entered in Anda's stake. Would Anda get nervous around so many other dogs? Esther held tightly to her leash. Anda sniffed the air. She could tell something important was going to happen.

The dogs had to retrieve on land and in water. Anda did best in the water, but her land trial was first. The birds were flushed. Esther heard the rifle blasts and saw the birds plunge to the ground. The judges watched carefully as the dogs went after them.

For a moment, Anda got lost going after a

43

Born swimmers, Labradors are happiest in the water.

downed bird. Esther shouted a quick command. Anda took only a moment to get back on track. In minutes she returned to Esther holding the bird gently in her mouth. Esther hugged and petted her. Because she had hesitated, she wouldn't get as many points. But she had still done an excellent job. Esther was proud.

Soon it was time for Anda's water trial. Esther could hardly contain her excitement. This was Anda's strongest event. Would she do well?

Once again the birds were flushed. The rifles fired, and the dogs were off. Anda was gone in a flash. She plunged into the icy lake and swam after a bird. In one scoop, her jaw closed around it. Esther hardly had time to think before Anda was dropping the bird at her feet. The crowd applauded. Esther hugged her dog tight, squeezing her hard in her happiness. But no one was quite as happy as Anda herself. The talented Labrador seemed to know that she had done well.

Many owners think the Lab is the world's most perfect dog.

GLOSSARY/ INDEX

Hip Dysplasia 18, 28—An inherited condition that affects a dog's hip joints.

Housebreak 23—To teach a dog to relieve itself on newspaper or outside the house.

Litter 16, 28—A family of puppies born at a single whelping.

Neuter 26—To remove a male dog's testes to prevent it from making female dogs pregnant.

Pedigree 18—A chart that lists a dog's ancestors.

Seeing Eye Dog 6—A dog specially trained to guide blind people.

Spay 26—To remove a female dog's ovaries to prevent pregnancy.

Stud 28—A purebred male used for breeding.

Teats 30—A female dog's nipples. Puppies suck on the teats to get milk.

Umbilical Cord 30—A hollow tube that carries nutrients to a puppy while it is in its mother's body.

Veterinarian 16, 22—A doctor trained to take care of animals.

Wean 33—To make a puppy stop drinking its mother's milk and eat solid food instead.

Whelping Box 30—A roomy box in which a female dog can give birth to her puppies.

Withers 11—A dog's shoulders; the point

where its neck joins the body. A dog's height is measured at the withers.

Worms 22—Parasites that live in a dog's intestines and can make it sick.